THE SMART ASS BOOK OF PUNS

Published by LEFD Designs
ISBN 978-0-6488601-0-5
www.lefddesigns.com

YOU WANNA PIZZA ME?!

DON'T BE
A PRICK

FULL MOON

YOU'RE BEING IRRELEPHANT

YOU MAKE ME FLUSH

WHATEVER TICKLES YOUR PICKLE

YOU HAVE GOAT TO BE KIDDING

DUCK OFF

ONE SHARKASTIC
SUN OF A BEACH

COMET ME, BRO

DON'T BE A
HIPPO-CRITE

YOU GIRAFFE
ME CRAZY

THAT FEELING WHEN ZE-BRA IS OFF

ARE EWE SERIOUS...

I SHIH-TZU NOT

YOU HAVE CAT TO BE KITTEN ME RIGHT MEOW

FOR FOX SAKE

BEARLY TOLERATING YOUR SARCASM

YOU'RE BOARING ME

TURDLE

DON'T BE
SO SHELLFISH

I'VE HAD ENOUGH
OF YOUR CRAB

I'M NOT AMOOSED WITH YOUR BULL

OTTER MY WAY, PUNK

TOO SOFISHTICATED FOR YOU

DONUT EVEN...

BEACH, PLEASE

THIS IS MY
MUFFIN TOP

I'M NOT FAT, I'M JUST
A LITTLE HUSKY

BAD PUNS ARE HOW EYE ROLL

ALSO AVAILABLE...

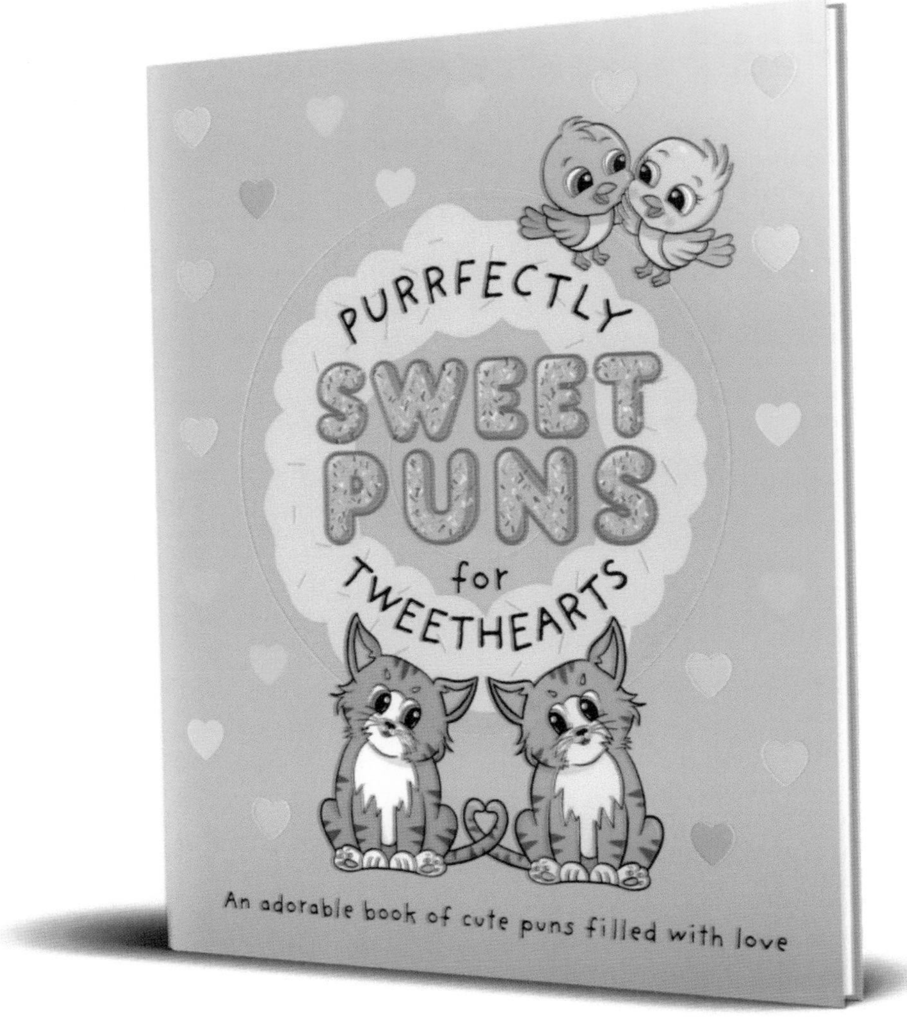

'PURRFECTLY SWEET PUNS FOR TWEETHEARTS'

LEFD

Designs

THE SMART ASS BOOK OF PUNS

WWW.LEFDDESIGNS.COM

Printed in Great Britain
by Amazon

23110244R00021